The Postmodern Bank Safety Net

The Postmodern Bank Safety Net

Lessons from Developed and Developing Economies

Charles W. Calomiris

The AEI Press

Publisher for the American Enterprise Institute
WASHINGTON, D.C.

1997

The author thanks Urs Birchler, Gerard Caprio, Geoffrey Wood, and seminar participants at the National Bank of Switzerland, the University of St. Gallen, and the University of Konstanz for comments on an earlier draft.

To order call toll free 1-800-462-6420 or 1-717-794-3800. For all other inquiries please contact the AEI Press, 1150 Seventeenth Street, N.W., Washington, D.C. 20036 or call 1-800-862-5801.

ISBN 978-0-8447-7100-7

1 3 5 7 9 10 8 6 4 2

THE AEI PRESS
Publisher for the American Enterprise Institute
1150 17th Street, N.W., Washington, D.C. 20036

Contents

Foreword

America's financial markets are in many respects the wonder of the world for their efficiency and dynamism. But they are also constrained by numerous obsolete regulatory policies, and their very dynamism makes them a tempting target for new political impositions. The U.S. government is awash in proposals to revise financial market regulation—in some cases to remove or streamline long-standing regulatory policies, in others to add new government controls. The stakes for the U.S. economy are considerable.

This pamphlet is one of a series of American Enterprise Institute studies of a broad range of current policy issues affecting financial markets, including regulation of the structure and prices of financial services firms; the appropriate role of government in providing a "safety net" for financial institutions and their customers; regulation of securities, mutual funds, insurance, and other financial instruments; corporate disclosure and corporate governance; and issues engendered by the growth of electronic commerce and the globalization of financial markets.

The AEI studies present important original research on trends in financial institutions and markets and objective assessments of legislative and regulatory proposals. Prepared by leading economists and other financial experts, and distributed to a wide audience of policy makers, financial executives, academics, and journalists, these studies aim to make the developing policy debates more informed, more empirical, and—we hope—more productive.

CHRISTOPHER DEMUTH
President
American Enterprise Institute

1

The Evolution of the Modern Financial Safety Net

This analysis of the government "safety net" for the financial system begins with a review of the changes that have taken place over the twentieth century in policies and attitudes. The first chapter discusses the period of expansion of protection from the 1930s to the early 1980s, which saw the construction of an extensive "modern" safety net. The second chapter shows how new evidence began to alter attitudes and policies in the mid-1980s, within the United States and other economies. In the third chapter, the analysis considers alternative solutions to the incentive problems of the safety net and compares the approach based on the 1988 Basle international bank capital standards and provisions of the Federal Deposit Insurance Corporation Improvement Act of 1991 with a potentially more promising approach to reforming government safety nets—one that relies on market discipline through a subordinated-debt-financing requirement. Chapter 4 reviews and evaluates two prominent examples of recent reform in the light of the arguments of chapter 3: namely, the experiences of Chile and Argentina, countries that have injected elements of private market discipline into their safety net reforms. Chapter 5 offers some conclusions.

Background

Before 1933, throughout the world the government's direct role as an insurer of financial stability was relatively modest. Indirectly—through monetary, fiscal, and debt-management policies—government actions sometimes contributed to stability or instability. Historically, the government also licensed (and in some cases owned significant stakes in) private financial institutions. But microeconomic government interventions—subsidized lending, insurance of private institutions' claims, or government recapitalization of particular institutions—were relatively uncommon.

In the United States, at first the Federal Reserve loaned reserves to banks only against high-quality collateral assets, a practice that rendered the Federal Reserve helpless in preventing the failures of banks whose depositors had lost faith in their solvency, since riskless lending (even at a subsidized rate) is of very limited value to a troubled institution financed by short-term (demandable) debt. The founders of the Federal Reserve did not perceive that as a deficiency, since they saw the Fed primarily as a vehicle for smoothing fluctuations in the seasonal supply of reserves and, consequently, seasonal movements in the riskless money market interest rate. To the extent that the Fed was to act as a lender of last resort during crises, its role was to expand the aggregate supply of reserves, not to provide subsidized lending against questionable collateral or to try to rescue banks. The Fed was not willing to lend to banks in a way that placed it in a junior position relative to banks' depositors. By being unwilling to accept risky bank loans of uncertain value as collateral, the Fed ensured that if depositors lost faith in the (unobservable) value of a bank's loan portfolio, that bank would fail.

In Britain, Bagehot's maxim for the lender of last resort—to lend freely at a penalty rate during a crisis—had inspired some limited government intervention during financial crises that went beyond Fed discount lending policy. The Bank of England's line of credit to the bank syndicate that bailed out Barings in 1890, for example, placed the Bank of England in a junior risk position relative to the depositors of the London banks. Such assistance was capable of better averting bank failures, since the lender of last resort was willing to take on default risk in a way that mitigated the incentives of depositors to withdraw funds from banks during uncertain times. It is worth emphasizing, however, that the assistance by the Bank of England placed it at minimal risk and *maximized the privatization of risk* during the crisis of 1890. The arrangement between the banks and the Bank of England placed the Bank of England in a senior position relative to the individual stockholders of the London banks, who were jointly liable for losses from the Barings bailout.

In many countries, especially since the nineteenth century, banks and governments had also acted as partners in special ways during wartime. Government sometimes relied on banks to assist in war finance in exchange for protection for the banks from failure if the value of government debt fell. And in some cases—for example, the protection afforded U.S. banks during the Civil War (Calomiris 1991)—the government used its power to define the numeraire in the economy (and to suspend convertibility of that numeraire into hard currency) to protect banks from adverse changes in the *government's* financial position.

Notwithstanding all these interventions, by modern (mid-to-late-twentieth-century) standards pre-1930s governments were skeptical of the merits of publicly managed and publicly funded assistance to financial institutions during peacetime. There is clear evidence that government stinginess was not the result of any ignorance of economic externalities associated with bank failures but rather reflected appreciation for the moral-hazard consequences of providing bailouts (Calomiris 1989, 1990, 1992, 1993a; Flood 1992). The primary sources of protection against the risk of depositor runs on a bank were other banks. That assistance was not guaranteed but rather depended on the willingness of private coalitions of bankers to provide protection to a threatened institution (Gorton 1985; Calomiris 1989,

1990; Calomiris and Gorton 1991; Calomiris and Schweikart 1991; Calomiris 1993b; Calomiris and Mason 1997).

Attitudes changed in the 1930s. In the United States, in 1932, President Hoover gave in to pressure to provide a new source of government lending to banks and other firms in distress: the Reconstruction Finance Corporation (RFC). Initially, the RFC, like the Fed, was authorized to lend only against high-quality collateral. In 1933, however, its authority was extended to permit the purchase of the preferred stock of banks and other firms. That change was important. RFC lending on high-quality collateral provided no subsidy to distressed institutions, and econometric analysis of the impact of such lending suggests that it did not prevent banks from failing. In contrast, preferred stock purchases did reduce the probability of failure for distressed institutions (Mason 1996). Collateral and eligibility requirements on Fed discount window lending were also relaxed in the wake of the depression (Schwartz 1992; Calomiris and Wheelock 1997).

In addition, federal deposit insurance—a concept that, before 1933, was viewed as a transparent attempt to subsidize small, high-risk banks—passed in 1933 as part of a complex political compromise between the House and Senate banking committees (Calomiris and White 1994). New programs to provide price supports for farmers and subsidized credit for mortgages, farms, small businesses, and other purposes followed, often justified by arguments that they would "stabilize" credit markets and limit unwarranted financial distress.

The Modern Age of Government Intervention

Thus began the modern age of government intervention to "stabilize" the financial system. By the 1950s and 1960s, many of the depression-era reforms had achieved the status of unquestionable wisdom. They constituted part of the new "automatic stabilizers" lauded by macroeconomists as insurance against a financial collapse like that of the 1930s. Deposit insurance protected banks from the discipline of the market—that is, from the possibility that depositors might force banks to fail or to contract their asset risk in response to portfolio losses. In doing so, deposit insurance ensured that the supply of loanable funds would not contract as much during recessions as it otherwise would. While that stabilizing aspect of deposit insurance protection was emphasized, macroeconomists neglected the destabilizing effect of the removal of market discipline—that is, the increased risk of financial collapse implied by the willingness of banks to assume greater risks in the wake of adverse shocks to their portfolios.

As late as the 1970s, evidence from the postwar period seemed to warrant that view, since there had been remarkably few failures of insured financial institutions. In retrospect, we now know that the 1950s and 1960s were an unusually stable period characterized by low commodity and asset price volatility. But many economists at the time attributed the economic stability of that period to the new stabilizing government safety net.

In the immediate post–World War II environment, many countries followed the lead of the United States in establishing aggressive financial safety nets. The new Bretton Woods institutions—the World Bank and the International Monetary Fund—were also conceived in the heady atmosphere of the late 1940s. Confidence was widespread that financial assistance from governments, or coalitions of governments, to absorb private default risk would pave the way for worldwide economic growth and stability.

The new financial safety net constructed in the 1930s remained essentially untested during the first forty years of its existence. The volatile environment of the 1970s and 1980s provided the first test. The shocks to asset prices, exchange rates, and commodity prices of the 1970s and 1980s reminded economists that volatility is the norm. More important, it eroded their optimism about the stabilizing effects of the financial safety net by demonstrating how drastically different the behavior of protected banks (and their regulators) could be once adverse shocks significantly weakened the banks' capital positions. The possibility that under adverse circumstances banks would consciously abuse the safety net, or that regulators and supervisors would consciously avoid their duty, seemed remote in the 1960s. The experience of the 1970s and 1980s changed those perceptions.

The 1970s undermined the confidence in macroeconomic "fine-tuning" that had reigned in the 1960s, but it was the 1980s and 1990s that saw a worldwide transformation in thinking about the stabilizing effects of the financial safety net. Initially, the bank failures in the United States seemed the result of exogenous influences—monetary policy and shocks to commodity prices. The rise in interest rates had placed much of the savings and loan industry into insolvency by 1982 (Barth and Bartholomew 1992). The combination of high oil prices, high interest rates, and the decline in dollar prices of commodities sent U.S. agriculture into a tailspin in the early 1980s. Related shocks to developing countries that were heavy borrowers, like Brazil, brought new challenges for sovereign borrowers and their banks. The 1982 collapse of oil prices sent new shock waves through oil-producing areas like Mexico, Texas, Oklahoma, and Venezuela as well as through the banks that had financed the oil exploration boom of the 1970s. Other countries were affected by a combination of commodity and asset price shocks. Chile's financial system, for example, faced unprecedented strain as the price of copper fell and later as U.S. interest rate rises of the early 1980s pulled foreign capital out of Chile and set the stage for the collapse of its fixed exchange rate.

Initially, the financial distresses of the early 1980s appeared to reinforce the argument for an aggressive safety net. The farm debt crisis that gripped U.S. farmers at that time brought calls for more subsidies, more lending, and debt moratoriums. In 1982, when distressed U.S. S&Ls cried out for regulatory relief, they received new powers to raise insured funds and to invest them in highly risky assets. They were also granted a new form of accounting (regulatory accounting principles) to avoid recognizing losses to capital when asset values fell. The crisis of developing-country debt also brought calls for moratoriums and for assistance from international agencies.

The first major American financial institution made insolvent through its exposure to oil price risk, Penn Square, was allowed to fail in 1982. But the U.S. government changed that policy in 1983, when Continental Illinois was faced with a "silent run" on its uninsured debt. Concluding that Continental was "too big to fail," the government decided to recapitalize the bank, thus protecting not only insured depositors but also uninsured claimants on the bank.

The Fed also participated to an unprecedented degree in discount window lending to insolvent financial institutions during the 1980s. That lending did not place the Fed at significant risk (since its special legal status gives it a senior, collateralized claim on bank assets), but it did allow insolvent institutions to continue to lend and meet their reserve requirements, while the government insurers of banks bore the burden of the continuing losses from permitting these so-called zombies to remain active. The Fed did so with the wholehearted approval of the Federal Deposit Insurance Corporation (FDIC), which hoped to postpone the realization of losses as long as possible, given the low level of its funds. The anticipated political costs of publicizing those losses (especially before the election of 1988) gave elected officials the incentive to encourage such "regulatory forbearance" on the part of the agencies that insured the losses of financial institutions (Kane 1989, 1992).

The pendulum of political support for such broad protection began to swing back in the mid-1980s. It became increasingly clear that financial risk was not all exogenous— much of it had been chosen by institutions and individuals that knew they were protected (at taxpayers' expense) from downside loss. The notion that the government was subsidizing risk, and consequently that financial institutions were purposefully increasing it, was viewed as late as the early 1980s as the unrealistic hypothesis of a handful of financial economists. In a matter of several years, however, amid mounting evidence that banks, with impunity, were deliberately taking risks, the minority critique became the consensus view, both in the United States and abroad.

Thus, many came to view the safety net—previously lauded as a risk reducer—as the single most important destabilizing influence in the financial system. It is interesting to review how that transformation in thinking came about and how it led to a new postmodern movement to reform the safety net.

2
Questioning the Safety of the Safety Net

The S&L crisis in the United States was of central importance in galvanizing the debate over safety net reform. It provided clear, sometimes sensational, evidence of ways in which government protection of financial institutions could be abused. The evidence that much of the loss experienced within the industry resulted from legal, voluntary risk taking and fraud (rather than exogenous shocks) had a particularly striking effect on the academic debate.

Barth and Bartholomew (1992) provided descriptive evidence of the mismanagement of the savings and loans that created the largest costs to taxpayers. Many of those losses were produced *after* these institutions had become insolvent. With little or no capital at stake, these institutions used the new powers granted them in 1982 to increase their asset risk and to grow at a phenomenal rate, financed by insured deposits. This costly strategy made sense from the standpoint of an insolvent S&L. Only a combination of rapid growth and high profits would restore the capital of the institution, providing it with a new lease on life.

The Moral-Hazard Problem

Horvitz (1992) drew attention to this "moral-hazard" problem in his analysis of the behavior of Texas banks and thrifts. He argued that losses of capital led these institutions to increase their asset risk (the opposite of prudent bank practice) because their low capital levels implied little risk of further loss and significant upside gains to bank stockholders. Texas institutions that experienced losses from financing oil exploration moved into the business of financing commercial real estate development, an even riskier version of their earlier failed "bet" on oil exploration. Texas banks and thrifts suffered some of their worst losses as the result of this second round of risk taking, *after* the exogenous decline in oil prices and bank capital had occurred.

Brewer (1995) provided formal evidence consistent with the arguments of Barth and Bartholomew, Horvitz, and others. He showed that capital losses had encouraged asset reallocation toward higher risk. More important, he showed that, for low-capital institutions, the decision to increase asset risk resulted in higher market value of the institution's stock. In other words, institutions taking advantage of the subsidization of risk offered by deposit insurance were creating value for their stockholders and were perceived as doing so in the stock market.

The evidence of abuse of the safety net by savings and loans provided legitimacy to economic arguments about perverse incentives from deposit insurance. It was no longer possible to argue that concerns about incentives were unrealistic, that bankers were simply the victims of exogenous shocks, or that bankers were not the sort to assume imprudent risk willingly just to increase expected profit.

Nor were savings and loan failures and the oil-related bank collapses in Texas and Oklahoma the only examples of moral-hazard costs from government risk subsidization. Carey (1990) analyzed the boom and bust in U.S. agricultural land and commodity prices and lending during the 1970s and 1980s and their relationship to government policies to provide "liquidity" to farmers. One of the legacies of the Great Depression was the Farm Credit System, a network of government-guaranteed financial institutions that specialize in mortgage and working capital lending to farmers. Somewhat like a lender of last resort, the Farm Credit

System has government protection and a mandate to maintain credit supply to farmers. It also imposes less demanding collateral standards for lending. Carey found a close relationship between government-sponsored credit (through the Farm Credit System) and excessive risk taking by farmers. The Farm Credit System was increasingly willing to lend against questionable collateral (land) during the boom, while private banks withdrew from the market as lending risk increased.

Interestingly, early twentieth century American financial history provides additional evidence of the moral-hazard costs of deposit insurance and the potential for insured (subsidized) bank lending to drive speculative booms in agricultural real estate. Calomiris (1989, 1990, 1993a) argues that state-level deposit insurance schemes in several states during and after World War I promoted unwarranted agricultural expansion during the war and extreme loss in the face of postwar declines in commodity and land prices.

As all this new evidence of moral hazard in banking mounted in the late 1980s, financial economists familiar with the savings and loan, oil-lending, and agricultural lending crises considered other areas of potential weakness in the incentive structure of the American financial system. The two most important potential areas of weakness were large commercial-center banks (covered by implicit, "too-big-to-fail" insurance) and life insurance companies (covered by state-level insurance schemes). Many of these institutions had experienced large losses in their commercial real estate portfolios, some of which followed tax law changes in 1986 that limited accelerated depreciation for commercial real estate transactions.

Some evidence suggests that life insurers and large banks that had experienced significant capital losses were shifting into high-risk assets under the cover of explicit or implicit insurance protection. Brewer and Mondschean (1993) and Brewer, Mondschean, and Strahan (1992) found evidence of moral hazard in the portfolio choices of life insurance companies reminiscent of Brewer's (1995) evidence for savings and loans. Boyd and Gertler (1994) found that the largest U.S. banks had loss rates on commercial loans five times those of small banks and loss rates on construction loans nearly ten times those of small banks (as of 1992). They argued that regional factors did not explain those differences and concluded that part, if not all, of the higher risk of large banks reflected the incentive to take risk offered by the too-big-to-fail doctrine.

While there was never a collapse of U.S. money-center banks or life insurers, one could argue that the collapse was only narrowly averted by the rebound in the economy after 1991. Several consecutive years of profits have now recapitalized these institutions, reduced their probabilities of failure, and thereby lessened their incentives to assume excessive risk. But in 1990 and 1991, some commentators claimed that some U.S. money-center banks were insolvent or near insolvent and that others were barely solvent and unable to borrow extensively on the federal funds market. If the recession had persisted into 1992 or 1993, it is conceivable that large U.S. banks and life insurance companies might have continued to increase their portfolio risk, experienced losses, and eventually been granted a massive bailout from federal and state governments.

Experiences of Other Countries

Thus far, I have focused on the U.S. experience, but the United States was not the scene of either the first or the worst case of financial collapse during the 1980s and 1990s.

Chile. The Chilean experience was arguably the first clear case of the two-stage pattern discussed above. A decline in copper prices, and other exogenous shocks that worsened Chile's position internationally, were followed by regulatory forbearance and government assumption of the risks in the banking system. That response promoted new risk taking by banks and their borrowers and culminated in the costly collapse of many financial institutions. One of the primary risks that engaged subsidized speculation was the risk of currency devaluation, which banks and their borrowers bet against heavily in 1981 and 1982. When devaluation came, the (government-assumed) losses were enormous.

As in many other countries, the adverse macroeconomic consequences of the initial exogenous shocks to the Chilean economy made it politically difficult to impose the necessary discipline on banks. As de la Cuadra (then minister of finance) and Valdes (1992, 75) argue,

> The superintendency could not include in its loan classification procedure a truly independent assessment of the exposure of bank debtors to foreign exchange and interest rate risk because such an assessment would have interfered with official macroeconomic policies.

De la Cuadra and Valdes go on to trace how excess risk taking by banks and firms, and eventual losses from those risks, produced economic devastation by 1982 and increasingly perverse incentives for lenders (pp. 79–80). Their discussion warrants substantial quotation:

> In 1981 most banks saw their effective capital plummet further as soon as optimistic debtors became less willing to pay when the net worth of their corporations fell. This reluctance reinforced the previous perverse incentives to banks, so that banks became even more willing to assume credit risks derived from exchange rate and interest rate risks.
>
> By 1981 financing decisions by Chilean firms and banks reflected a *de facto* government guarantee to the private sector for foreign exchange risk. Our analysis has identified the superintendency's lack of penalization of credit risk in its loan classification criteria as the channel for the guarantee.
>
> The outcome of this structural contingent sub-

sidy was that many small and medium-sized businesses got deeply into debt in 1981. Debts to banks increased during 1981 from 37.6 percent to 50.4 percent of GDP [gross domestic product] in response to the rise in real interest rates. . . .

By mid-1982 the fall in GDP was so steep that it took on the character of a depression. In June 1982 the government finally decided to devalue the exchange rate by 14 percent. . . . By the end of 1982 the losses that the devaluations had inflicted on the holders of dollar-denominated debts had created insolvency among firms of all sizes. . . .

The sorry state of most debtors caused delinquent loans to rise from 2.3 percent of loans in December 1981 to 3.83 percent in February 1982 and 6.31 percent in May. Most delinquent loans turned out to be 100 percent losses, so they reduced the net worth of banks. . . .

On July 12, 1982, the central bank decided to allow banks to defer their losses over several years, so it began to buy the banks' delinquent loan portfolios at face value. The banks, however, had to promise to repurchase the portfolios at face value over time with 100 percent of their profits, so the scheme did not improve bank solvency by itself. It solved a liquidity problem but also set the stage for making good the implicit contingent subsidy that the government had offered to speculators in 1981.

The authors proceed to emphasize that loans to industrial firms linked to banks through conglomerates were especially forthcoming from banks as a consequence of the government subsidization of risk. Thus, despite its free market orientation and stated commitment to private discipline in banking, Chile ended up insuring "uninsured" claims on banks, subsidizing high-risk resurrection strategies on the part of its banks, and passing on enormous risk-encouraging credit subsidies to large industrial firms with close links to banks.

The Chilean and U.S. examples were followed by a wave of banking disasters in other countries, against which the banking collapses of the 1930s pale by comparison. Many of the cases bear a strong resemblance to the Chilean and U.S. examples. Recent surveys by Caprio and Klingebiel (1996a, 1996b) and Lindgren, Garcia, and Saal (1996) have demonstrated how widespread the problem of moral hazard has become in the financial system, spanning the globe and including developed and developing economies. The lessons they draw from these experiences are uniform: well-intentioned government lenders of last resort (or insurers of deposits) have promoted both large dead-weight losses (from inefficient investments and restructuring costs) and enormous fiscal strains on governments. Crises also seem to have an important disruptive effect on postcrisis growth and investment rates, probably through the destruction of institutional and human capital in the banking system.

Government-Industry Partnerships. A common denominator of the Chilean, Venezuelan, Mexican, and Japanese crises—each estimated to cost in excess of 10 percent of its country's gross domestic product—is the extent to which the banking disaster, and the unwillingness of government to allow banks to suffer the consequences of their own losses, resulted from a close "partnership" between large industrial groups (which controlled the major banks) and the government. These bank-affiliated groups can take on the status of semipublic institutions. They maintain enormous influence over government policy and see government protection of banks as a key dimension of their relationship with government.

With the exception of Chile, these countries' banking crises were "resolved" without addressing the moral-hazard problems that underlay them. In Venezuela, despite a commitment not to bail out banks, banks were bailed out at enormous cost when regulators faced political pressure to do so (de Krivoy 1995). Nothing has been done to avoid the repetition of a similar crisis in the future.

Mexico. In Mexico, the large banks were privatized in 1991, auctioned at a very high price to the country's largest industrialists. Mexican banks expanded their lending and portfolio risk on a virtually nonexistent capital base. By 1993, the banking system was viewed as unstable if not insolvent and posed the threat of a large potential fiscal drain on the government. The banks' weak financial conditions, losses on derivative positions abroad, and their knowledge of their own potential impact on the Mexican government's ability to maintain its exchange rate policy led the banks themselves to initiate the run on the peso in 1994. They chose to liquidate their highly speculative bets against devaluation (Garber 1997). The similarities to the Chilean experience are uncanny.

Despite the clear moral-hazard lessons from the Mexican crisis, the political interests of the U.S. Treasury Department (which had expressed enormous confidence in precrisis Mexico), the Mexican government, and its foreign lenders have been best served by misinterpreting the peso crisis as an unwarranted run, resulting from a "liquidity" problem that was produced by the short maturity structure of government debt, and self-fulfilling adverse expectations. The U.S.-sponsored bailout of the Mexicans, partly in consequence of the absolution that accompanied it, has done little to improve the root causes of the crisis, including the structure of the banking system. Some accounting reforms have taken place, some new foreign entry into banking has been allowed, and some recognition of loan losses (paid for by the government) has begun. But nothing has been done to limit the future abuse of government insurance, which insures virtually all liabilities in the Mexican financial system.

Japan. The Japanese banking system has hidden its losses behind a veil of regulatory forbearance for several years, hoping that improvement in economic performance will pay for bank loan losses. An outright bailout of the banking system would be unpopular in Japan, so forbearance has been the option of least political resistance. Of course, that solution ignores the incentive that low-capital institutions face to take on new risks. Thus, the costs of the bailout may grow over time, even as economic conditions improve.

Unlike Venezuela, Mexico, and Japan, Chile moved aggressively, as early as 1986, to recognize and resolve the underlying incentive problems that had produced its financial crisis (see the detailed discussion in chapter 4). Other countries—including the United States, Argentina, El Salvador, New Zealand, and Malaysia—also began to take seriously some of the lessons of moral hazard and regulatory forbearance that underlie the many recent examples of financial crises.

The Basle Standards

The period 1988–1993 witnessed unprecedented actions internationally, especially in the United States, to limit safety net protection of banks. The passage of the Basle international bank capital standards in 1988, imposing crude, risk-based capital standards on insured institutions, was the first step. It was followed in the United States with the Financial Institutions Reform, Recovery and Enforcement Act of 1989 (FIRREA) (implementing the standards and adding new limits on the activities insured by institutions) and the Federal Deposit Insurance Corporation Improvement Act (FDICIA) in 1991 (establishing guidelines for "prompt corrective action" to enforce the new standards).

The 1991 law also codified a limited version of the too-big-to-fail doctrine, but its intent was to limit its application. Under the 1991 law, for insurance to be extended to "uninsured" bank liabilities (beginning in 1995), the FDIC, the secretary of the Treasury (in consultation with the president), and a supernumerary majority of the boards of the FDIC and the Federal Reserve must agree that not doing so "would have serious adverse effects on economic conditions or financial stability." Moreover, if uninsured deposits are covered under this provision, the insurance fund must be reimbursed through emergency special assessments. Because the nation's largest banks would end up paying a disproportionate cost of such a bailout, advocates of FDICIA argued that the large banks could be relied on to lobby successfully against the extension of insurance to uninsured deposits, unless the criterion for assistance was truly met. Finally, in 1993, the Fed put in place new restrictions on discount window lending to limit its lending to distressed banks and avoid a repetition of its complicity in regulatory forbearance during the 1980s.

Despite the progress that has been made in the United States, one can question whether these new and better government rules, implemented by government regulators and supervisors, are really a promising approach to resolving incentive problems attendant to the financial safety net. Do government supervisors possess the skill and the incentive to identify capital losses in banks as diligently as private market agents would, with their own money on the line? Will supervisors or regulators be tempted to ignore losses when it is politically expedient for them, or their superiors, to do so? Are existing measures of asset risk, or existing requirements for various types of capital, likely to result in prudent risk taking by banks, even if the new capital standards are enforced properly?

Clearly, opportunities for increasing risk in ways not captured by the Basle standards—particularly through exchange rate and interest rate derivatives—pose an important problem in this regard. I will also argue that an emphasis on equity capital, as opposed to subordinated debt capital, is an important weakness of the Basle approach. Doubts about the efficacy of the Basle-FDICIA approach to ensuring that the safety net is not abused have produced alternative approaches to managing safety net protection, to which we now turn.

3

The Postmodern Safety Net

The motivation for what I call the postmodern safety net is to avoid abuse of government protection that arises when the cost to banks for access to the safety net does not properly reflect their decisions to bear risk. Any meaningful reform of deposit insurance must either credibly restrict risk taking or make the cost of protection against losses to bank deposits sensitive to the riskiness of insured deposits. Doing either would remove any incentive for banks to increase risk in response to a capital loss, since they would receive no subsidy from raising their risk.

Figure 3–1 plots a deposit isorisk line for a ten-basis-point default risk premium on bank deposits (as a point of reference), using the Black-Scholes option pricing formula to map from the combination of bank asset risk and bank leverage to the actuarially fair default (and insurance) premium on deposits (see Calomiris and Wilson 1997 for further discussion of contingent claims models of bank liabilities). The intuition for figure 3–1 is clear: the default risk on bank debt is a positive function of both asset risk and leverage. For a bank operating at point A (on the ten-basis-point deposit isorisk line) the fair insurance premium on deposits (if the government insures all deposits) would be ten basis points. Banks would pay the riskless rate of interest to depositors and ten basis points to the government. If banks increased their asset risk (moving to point B in figure 3–1), then the fair deposit insurance premium would rise to twenty basis points. So long as the government actually raises the insurance premium by ten basis

FIGURE 3–1
DEPOSIT RISK AS A FUNCTION OF ASSET RISK AND LEVERAGE

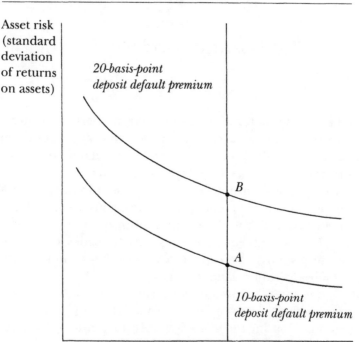

Asset risk (standard deviation of returns on assets)

20-basis-point deposit default premium

B

A

10-basis-point deposit default premium

Ratio of bank assets to bank capital

points whenever banks move from A to B, banks will have no incentive to increase asset risk.

The Problem

The problem is, however, that government supervisors and regulators may not behave ideally, either because they do not know the bank's true deposit default risk or because they face political incentives to ignore it. With respect to the first problem, recall that the unique characteristic of bank lending is the private information that banks have about the value of their credit risks. Bank loans are costly for outsiders to value because doing so requires detailed understanding of the fundamental credit risks of firms that borrow from banks (many of which are not well known to outsiders), as well as an understanding of how to value the bank's claims on the firm, which typically entail a variety of idiosyncratic covenants and collateral provisions.

If banks can hide increases in deposit default risk— either by hiding loan losses or disguising the riskiness of their portfolio—they can thereby avoid commensurate increases in insurance costs and obtain subsidies for increasing deposit risk. How do unregulated banking systems solve this "agency" problem? How do uninsured depositors ensure that they are paid an adequate yield to compensate for the default risk they bear?

Clearly, the problem was not solved historically, and should not be solved today, by making banks' credit risks costlessly transparent. Doing so would require extreme restrictions on bank activities. The social value of banking arises from banks' specializing in information creation and contract enforcement (the so-called delegated-monitoring function of banks). Although this delegation makes it costly for outsiders to monitor the riskiness of bank assets, such intermediation is highly productive since it economizes on the costs of information and control by creating banks that specialize in these activities.

The historical solution to the agency problem is to be found in the contracting structure of banks and the incentives that structure creates in an unregulated banking system. Calomiris and Kahn (1991) and Calomiris, Kahn, and Krasa (1994) argue that banks operate as three-party arrangements bringing together "insiders" (bank stockholder-managers), "informed outsiders" (large depositors that specialize in monitoring bank activities), and "uninformed depositors" (passive, small depositors). The uninformed rely on the informed depositors to monitor the banker. The "first-come, first-served" rule for deposit withdrawals, along with a sufficient amount of bank reserves, provides payoffs to informed monitors in "bad" states of the world that induce them to invest in information about bank activities and to run the bank if they see a sufficiently bad state of the world. The threat of an informed run, or an actual informed run, obviates agency (moral-hazard) costs that would otherwise arise from the fact that bankers have private information about the quality of their assets.

Because bank regulators and supervisors do not face strong incentives to invest in information (as would private depositors), it is less likely that they will be as well informed about the true risk characteristics of bank assets. Moreover, political considerations may make regulators and supervisors unwilling to penalize banks for increasing their risk, even if the authorities can observe that an increase in risk or a decline in bank capital has taken place. This tendency is particularly compelling during recession-induced bank "capital crunches" when politicians and regulators face strong incentives to "forbear" from strict enforcement of bank regulations to promote a larger supply of bank credit in the economy. The politically mandated forbearance of recent years—in the United States, Chile, Venezuela, Mexico, Japan, and elsewhere—provides little evidence that regulators can be relied on to control politically powerful bankers, especially when governments face populist pressures to expand credit supply during a downturn.

In contrast, private, uninsured depositors can be counted on to penalize banks for asset risk or leverage increases that produce higher default risk on deposits. Calomiris and Wilson (1997) find that New York City banks in the 1920s and 1930s faced strong pressure from depositors to limit default risk and that this pressure contributed to banks' decisions to shed risky loans during the 1930s.[1] Those same pressures are visible today. Continental Illinois was effectively forced into the hands of the government in 1984 by a "silent run" on the part of its uninsured deposi-

---

1. New York City banks received very little protection from deposit insurance during the 1930s, since very few of their deposits were small enough to qualify for insurance.

tors. Bank One faced the threat of similar problems temporarily in the mid-1990s, owing to the complexity of its derivatives positions and doubts by some of its creditors about the value and risk of those derivatives positions. To avoid private discipline, Bank One's executives met creditors privately for several days to explain their positions and reassure them, which they succeeded in doing.

The importance of asymmetric information (the lack of transparency of bank risk to outsiders) deserves emphasis. In the absence of asymmetric information (which makes it necessary for someone to invest credibly in monitoring bank risk and leverage), there would be no incentive problem in the safety net. The regulation of bank risk could be accomplished easily because deposit risk would be costlessly observable to everyone. But without asymmetric information, there would also be no need for banks, much less a bank safety net. Ironically, the very information problems that give rise to banks and to the desire for a safety net (to avoid banking panics) make it very difficult to ensure that the bank safety net will be incentive-compatible.[2]

Thus, minimum capital requirements (which underlie the Basle standards and the recent American and Chilean reforms) offer an inadequate solution to safety net incentive problems. Capital standards fail to prevent the subsidization of risk for two reasons. First, book capital standards constrain risk only so long as regulators and supervisors ensure that book capital bears a close relationship to true capital (that is, the implied market value of capital). But if bank losses are either not observed or not reported by supervisors, then capital standards may have little force. Second, even if regulators enforce capital requirements by fully recognizing capital losses whenever they occur, capital standards alone do not obviate safety net subsidies for risk taking.

---

2. Calomiris (1994) argues that, similarly, in the absence of asymmetric information problems, there would be no role for a central bank discount window to deal with financial problems occurring outside the banking system.

To see why this is so, consider the vertical line running through points A and B in figure 3–1. The vertical line representing a minimal required (market) capital ratio does not limit asset risk or default risk on deposits. Both points A and B satisfy the capital constraint; yet the fair premium for deposit insurance at point B is twenty basis points, while at point A it is ten basis points. Fully insured bank depositors will lend to banks at the riskless rate irrespective of bank risk. Thus, so long as deposit insurance premiums do not fully reflect asset risk choices by banks, bank profits will be an increasing function of asset risk.

The Solution

The deficiencies of minimum capital requirements have led to continuing calls for further reforms to deposit insurance within the United States and elsewhere. Two of the most popular reforms that have been considered are "narrow banking" and "market discipline" (or required "subordinated debt").

The narrow-banking approach would restrict government insurance to a separately chartered narrow bank within the bank holding company, which would hold transparently low-risk, market-priced assets and would issue insured deposits. The rest of the bank holding company's operations would be unregulated, and deposits held outside the narrow bank would be restricted to uninsured time deposits. Narrow banking effectively eliminates any risk to the government from insuring deposits and is thus simply another name for the suggestion that deposit insurance be repealed.

I have argued elsewhere (Calomiris 1997) that, even if the repeal of deposit insurance were desirable on economic grounds (assuming, for example, that private coalitions of bankers could provide most or all of the social gains contemplated by a government-run safety net), narrow banking is not politically credible. Uninsured short-term deposits outside the narrow bank would still leave banks susceptible to capital crunches and to the logical possibility of runs, which could be used to motivate ad hoc government interventions to protect uninsured deposits. Thus, narrow banking does not repeal deposit insurance but simply repeals all the prudential regulation and supervision that accompanies deposit insurance.

A subordinated-debt-financing requirement can provide an alternative means of reforming deposit insurance. It has the advantage of ensuring incentive compatibility with a minimal set of regulatory guidelines and no reliance on government supervisors to analyze and disclose the condition of bank loan portfolios.

Consider a rule that would require banks to finance a minimal fraction (say, 2 percent) of their total nonreserve assets with subordinated debt (uninsured certificates of deposit) earning a yield no greater than fifty basis points above the riskless rate.[3] That rule would force banks to operate below the fifty-basis-point risk schedule. If the most junior 2 percent of debt bears a premium of fifty basis points, then overall the fairly priced risk premium for all debt (including the 98 percent of debt that is insured) must be lower.

To be willing to hold the bank's debt, private subordinated-debt holders would have to be satisfied that the leverage and the portfolio risk of the bank were sufficiently low to warrant that low (fifty-basis-point) yield spread on debt. Banks that were unable to convince debt markets of the adequacy of their capital and the prudence of their investments would be unable to roll over some of their subordi-

---

3. Off-balance-sheet activities could be included in the measure of total nonreserve assets, as is done currently in computing "risk-weighted assets" under the Basle guidelines. Because the private market pricing of subordinated-debt issues of banks takes all risks into account (including on-balance-sheet credit risk, off-balance-sheet credit risk, and market risks), the difficulty of ascertaining or limiting off-balance-sheet risks is a further motivation for reliance on subordinated debt.

nated debt. Thus, the subordinated-debt-ratio requirement naturally pushes banks to reduce their portfolio risk if it ever becomes excessive.[4]

The limitation on the yield spread serves the important purpose of limiting the risk on insured debt (which is senior to the subordinated debt), and it may also be of some help in allowing one to set deposit insurance premiums close to an actuarially fair rate—that is, one that reflects the true risk of default on insured deposits. Contingent-claims pricing (based on the Black-Scholes model or some more realistic variant of that approach) can be used to derive the risk premium for insured debt from the observed yield on the subordinated debt.

In a world of growing complexity and expanding opportunities for rapid increases in portfolio risk (through derivatives or emerging-market securities), the most desirable feature of a reliance on subordinated-debt requirements is that they place the primary "regulatory" and "supervisory" burdens on sophisticated market participants with their own money at stake. Government regulators and supervisors have neither adequate skills nor sufficient incentives to monitor continuously and control the condition of banks.

Subordinated debt—or similar means of bringing private market discipline to bear on bank risk and capital choices—offers the only desirable solution to safety net incentive problems. The undesirable alternative is draconian restrictions on bank activities that try to limit risk taking by banks, in lending and elsewhere. In today's complex and competitive global banking environment, efficiency in banking is increasingly identified with broadening bank powers to enter new areas (Calomiris and Ramirez 1996). Extreme restrictions on bank risk taking not only undermine the lending function of banks but also translate into inefficient

---

4. The details of my subordinated-debt proposal can be found in Calomiris (1997). There I argue that overlapping generations of subordinated debt provide the most politically feasible means of credibly enforcing the subordinated-debt requirement.

limitations on the menu of services banks can offer.

This volume is not the first to note the advantages of subordinated-debt requirements over other ways to implement deposit insurance. The Federal Reserve Banks of Chicago and Atlanta developed detailed proposals for implementing subordinated-debt rules in the late 1980s, which were greeted favorably within and outside the Federal Reserve System (Keehn 1989; Wall 1989).

Nevertheless, subordinated debt did not win the day politically in the United States, nor in the international debate over capital standards. In the case of the United States, the late 1980s were a time of high loan losses and scarce capital in banking, and banks lobbied successfully against increasing market discipline through an uninsured-debt requirement.

Not only does the Basle (and the American) approach to capital standards avoid any subordinated-debt requirement, but it discriminates against subordinated debt. The Basle standards limit the extent to which tier-two capital components can satisfy total capital requirements, and also limit the extent to which subordinated debt can be used in the place of preferred stock to satisfy a tier-two capital requirement.

Of course, there are pitfalls that must be avoided if subordinated debt is to promote private market discipline and eliminate the moral-hazard problem posed by the government safety net. The two most important potential problems are (1) the potential for a politically motivated "bailout" of subordinated-debt holders; and (2) the potential for subordinated debt to be purposely overpriced by bank insiders who surreptitiously hold the debt. While both of these problems are serious, easily implemented safeguards can address them.

The potential for a bailout of subordinated debt, of course, would undermine the whole effort to eliminate the moral-hazard problem of deposit insurance, which rests on the imposition of losses (so-called haircuts) on uninsured-debt holders. If subordinated debt is not really junior to the government insurer, then it serves no purpose. It is widely believed that many governments provide implicit insurance for some or all uninsured debts in their banking systems. That raises the question of whether government is willing or able to allow private market discipline to take place.

In previous work (Calomiris 1997), I have argued that there are ways to limit the likelihood of a bailout of subordinated debt by restricting the identities of the holders of subordinated debt to those that the government would be unlikely to bail out (for example, foreign-based banks) and by providing other systemic protections to the financial system that limit the incentive to provide bailouts. Of course, there is no way to design a foolproof system of subordinated debt that can absolutely tie the hands of a government to permit private losses. That is not just a problem for subordinated-debt proposals to reform deposit insurance; a government that will always bail out everyone will not be able to design any means for avoiding the subsidization of risk.

The second potential problem with a subordinated-debt system is the potential for hidden, insider holdings of subordinated debt. Bank insiders would have an incentive to bid too high a price for subordinated debt, if they were permitted to do so. Since the banker is simply paying the excessive price to himself, he is indifferent to the loss from overpaying for the debt. But the banker gains from the lower cost of deposit insurance, which results from the government's reliance on private market pricing to constrain and measure bank risk taking. Thus, if insiders were permitted to hold subordinated debt, the yield paid for subordinated debt might bear little relationship to its true risk and might be of little use in eliminating the problem of moral hazard.

A simple solution to this problem is to require that the holders of subordinated debt have no direct or indirect interest in the stock of the bank that issues the debt. The requirement that subordinated-debt holders be unrelated foreign financial institutions might go a long way toward resolving the potential for insider holdings. Criminal and civil penalties for violating restrictions on the identities of subordinated-debt holders would also be useful.

The idea of subordinated debt as a cure to abuse of the safety net has important historical precedents. As much of the recent research on the operation of banks before the era of deposit insurance has emphasized, holders of large amounts of bank debt (often other banks) helped to ensure the proper mixture of assistance and discipline within the banking system (Gorton 1985; Calomiris 1989, 1990, 1993b; Calomiris and Gorton 1991; Calomiris and Schweikart 1991; Calomiris and Mason 1997). They provided mutual assistance to solvent banks during times of illiquidity because they were knowledgeable about the banks' prospects and because debt holders faced strong incentives to help solvent banks. They also provided discipline to insolvent banks by helping to hasten their closure when that was warranted, again because large debt holders were able to observe the condition of banks and because they faced a strong incentive to limit their losses as creditors.

4

Limited Progress in Chile and Argentina

Chile after 1986

Chile's banking collapse of 1982 predated by several years that of the United States. Chilean reforms—realized through a series of laws from November 1986 to August 1989 (Ramirez and Rosende 1992; Brock 1992, appendixes I and II; Budnevich 1996)—also predate the banking reform legislation of 1989 and 1991 in the United States. Those reforms followed an enormous government-financed bank recapitalization program, which ended in 1986. The banking collapse and the costs of recapitalization produced a strong consensus to prevent a recurrence of the banking collapse by strengthening regulation and supervision.

Like the reforms that took place later in the United States, Chile reformed its capital requirements and sought ways to improve the credibility of government supervision and regulation. Like FDICIA, Chile's new laws emphasized the importance of early intervention by the government to shut down low-capital institutions. The Chileans did more than the United States, however, to ensure that capital requirements would be meaningful and enforced by regulators by bringing the private market into the supervisory process.

They adopted aggressive market value accounting and required private supervision (auditing) of banks in addition to government supervision. Financial investments with more than a one-year maturity have to be repriced every month and marked to market. In addition to government supervision of internal risk ratings and valuations by the bank, two independent private auditors must examine each bank every year, and the results of their investigation are a matter of public record.

Reserve requirements are also high for Chilean banks. Demand deposits are subject to a 9 percent reserve requirement, and all deposits in excess of 2.5 times bank capital accounts must be backed by a 100 percent reserve deposit at the central bank. A special reserve requirement of 30 percent is placed on foreign deposits (which are presumed to be more prone to withdrawal).

The Chilean reforms also rolled back deposit insurance coverage, in a manner similar in effect to requiring some subordinated debt. Time deposits in banks receive only partial coverage, which means that, on the margin, private debt holders bear significant risk and therefore retain the incentive to monitor banks and punish imprudent behavior.

Central bank lending to commercial banks is limited to 60 percent of the total amount of required reserves, and the cost of borrowing is a steeply increasing function of the amount borrowed. Most important, borrowing from the central bank cannot free a bank from having to comply with reserve and capital regulations.

The superintendency is required to publish in a national newspaper three times per year a detailed report on each bank's compliance with capital requirements and the quality ratings of the bank's assets (which reflects explicit estimates of the probabilities of loss on those assets). The superintendency is explicitly forbidden by law from delaying the recognition of losses in a bank's accounts. Regulators' opinions are a matter of public record. The only right of secrecy within the banking system is the right of depositor privacy.

If a bank is found to be in violation of its capital or liquidity requirements, its shareholders must immediately raise capital to comply with the law. Banks that cannot recapitalize must be closed, unless both their uninsured creditors and the superintendency (which insures deposits) agree to restructure the bank. Because subordinated-debt holders must approve any restructuring of banks and because restructuring plans must be approved very quickly after the bank sinks below its minimum capital and reserve requirements, there is little opportunity or incentive for low-capital banks to adopt high-risk strategies after losing capital, since doing so would increase the incentive of subordinated-debt holders to block a restructuring of the bank's liabilities to avoid liquidation.

If the uninsured-debt holders of the bank are unwilling to rescue it, then the law permits a consortium of other private banks to make an uninsured loan to the weak bank, which can be used to satisfy the weak bank's capital requirement. The law is specifically designed to permit banks to limit negative externalities from systemic risks and envisions banks' establishing private regulatory clauses restricting the activities of the bank receiving assistance as part of the lending contract that preserves the institution.

Chilean law also emphasizes fire walls that legally separate the financing and risks of insured banks from those of nondepository affiliates. Furthermore, banks are not permitted to hold stock in firms. While these regulations limit some potential economies of scope from mixing banking, investment banking, and commerce (Calomiris and Ramirez 1996), they have the important benefit of limiting the potential abuse of deposit insurance. As the experience of many countries has taught, permitting banks to own industrial conglomerates can concentrate political power to such an extent that it undermines the political will of government to enforce banking regulations. This in turn makes it possible for bank-industry conglomerates to abuse the financial safety net.

Despite many desirable and innovative features of the Chilean approach, in its essence it is still a capital-cum-intervention scheme for reforming the safety net and is thus not very different in intent from the Basle-FDICIA approach. Because the political credibility of "partial" insurance is suspect, one could argue that there is no required subordinated debt financing. Neither is there any limit on the yield on uninsured bank deposits. The private audits mandated by law may be of some help, but one can question whether licensed auditors have the same strong incentives to discover and react to adverse information that subordinated-debt holders have.

Still, the Chilean approach does better than FDICIA at putting protections in place that keep low- (or negative-) capital banks from abusing deposit insurance protection. The removal of privacy protections for bank borrowers, the stated commitment to the aggressive application of mark-to-market accounting, the requirement of independent audits, legal prohibitions on forbearance, and the involvement of uninsured-debt holders in the resolution of bank distress are all intended to promote credible capital regulation. But, as shown in figure 3–1, even if these provisions help mitigate the problem of enforcing capital standards, that does not translate into removing the potential for abuse of the safety net because bank portfolio risk must also be controlled. That is especially worrying in an environment where derivatives and other important financial instruments offer the opportunities for banks to increase the riskiness of their portfolios arbitrarily (see also Edwards 1996, 164–67).

The Chilean bank regulations reflect an understanding of this problem. In addition to capital requirements, bank regulations limit or prohibit a variety of activities. Indeed, one could argue that the possibility for abuse of the safety net is not the largest social cost that comes from the Chilean approach. Of greater importance may be the cost of restricting the scope, complexity, and resourcefulness of banks. Such costly limits are deemed necessary because of the potential for abuse of the safety net under the Chilean capital-cum-intervention approach to reform: allowing banks to pursue arbitrarily large, hard-to-measure portfolio risks allows the possibility of abuse of the safety net.

Argentina

Argentina experienced three waves of costly banking collapses in the 1980s: 1980–1982, 1985, and 1989. Combined with the continuing problems of poor macroeconomic growth and hyperinflation, these financial crises helped to propel reforms in the 1990s. Argentina adopted some of the reforms introduced in Chile, including strict disclosure requirements about bank credit quality. But unlike Chile, Argentina opted for a more radical approach to banking reform. In 1992, deposit insurance was abolished (Miller 1993). Some government-controlled financial institutions remained beyond the grasp of private market discipline, but private banks (which comprise the bulk of the financial system and include domestic banks of various sizes as well as large, global players like Deutsche Bank, BNP, Citibank, Bank of Boston, and ABN Amro) were left to their own devices.

At the same time, as part of the same ambitious program of financial liberalization and fiscal austerity, Argentina adopted a currency board, effectively relinquishing power to determine the domestic money supply. The role of the monetary authority became converting pesos and dollars into one another on demand. The banking system was permitted to offer deposits in either pesos or dollars (which trade at par with one another).

Relinquishing monetary powers meant giving up the power to lend to banks through the discount window. Thus, by the early 1990s, Argentina had legislated away its ability to provide any government assistance to private banks through deposit insurance or central bank lending. When the Mexican "tequila crisis" hit in 1994 and 1995, Argentina experienced massive outflows of deposits, initially confined to peso-denominated accounts (reflecting a lack of confidence in Argentina's currency board commitment).

As the money supply imploded under the pressure of currency speculation and the economy began to falter, depositors' attention shifted to the (endogenous) problem of credit quality in the banking system.

Some banks experienced large outflows of deposits, and the government allowed some of those banks to fail. But as the crisis wore on, the government began to soften its stand a bit, responding to growing political pressures. It provided open bank assistance to subsidize acquisitions of some troubled banks, and it reintroduced deposit insurance, although limiting it to small accounts.

Studies of the banking crisis undertaken at the central bank indicated that the withdrawals of deposits from banks had not been random or irrational (Schumacher 1997). The banks most likely to lose deposits and fail were those that were demonstrably weakest before the crisis. At the same time, it also seemed that in at least one or two cases, solvent banks had faced withdrawals that forced their closure. Thus, while the Argentines came away from the crisis with substantial confidence in the wisdom of private market discipline over banks, they also felt that there was a need to enhance the government's role in avoiding unnecessary liquidation.

Three important initiatives emerged from the experience of 1994–1995. First, to improve its ability to provide liquidity to the financial system (without changing its commitment to a currency board), the government sought and arranged lines of credit from a consortium of international banks to be used in times of crisis. Those lines of credit are now in place and would permit "fiscally financed" (as opposed to monetary) discount window lending during a crisis.

Second, the government turned its attention to the promotion of institutional reforms that would enhance credit risk transparency for banks and their loan customers and thus possibly reduce potential problems of information asymmetry that promote unwarranted withdrawals from banks. Those reforms included a new bankruptcy code, a new initiative that will result in the centralization of collateral registration for bank loans, and a centralized public database to publicize the fundamental characteristics of bank borrowers and the credit risks they pose for individual banks.

Finally, in November 1996, a new law was passed in Argentina requiring banks to finance 2 percent of their total deposits in the form of subordinated debt. To my knowledge, Argentina is the only country to have instituted such a requirement. The subordinated-debt requirement ensures that, even if a bank's other deposits are all insured, at least 2 percent of its financing must satisfy the standards of the private market.

Unfortunately, the law has not instituted all the provisions envisioned in chapter 3. There is no maximum yield on subordinated debt, the identities of debt holders are not limited as proposed in chapter 3, and there is no attempt to link observed yields and the pricing of deposit insurance. One interpretation of the Argentine initiative is that it is an experiment to see how difficult it will be to create a new market for subordinated debt and to observe the yield structure of that market, before setting maximum yields and before relying too much on subordinated-debt yields to determine insurance premiums.

Despite this modest beginning, Argentina's approach may open a new chapter in the history of deposit insurance, one in which private market discipline acts in concert with government protection to allow incentive-compatible financial liberalization. The exciting prospect is that credible market discipline will permit banks to enter a richer array of activities without the fear that doing so will produce abuse of the safety net.

The other exciting dimension to Argentina's experiment is the separation of the financing of the lender of last resort from the monetary authority. Argentina hopes to maintain protection against liquidity shocks through borrowing from banks rather than through money creation (which would violate its currency board commitment). Of course, both access to credit lines and the credibility of the currency board depend crucially on perceptions of the long-run fiscal credibility of the government.

A critical factor that has allowed Argentina to embark on this ambitious program of reforms is its historical openness to foreign banks. The presence of many important global banks in Argentina matters in several ways. It applies pressure on domestic banks to become competitive. It brings large, diversified banks into the economy that can provide stability during difficult macroeconomic times. And it helps to make sensible bank regulation and supervisory discipline easier, since bank-government relations are naturally more at arm's length. New Zealand's banking system is a more extreme case of an almost entirely foreign-owned banking system, which displays a similar commitment to regulatory discipline.

The recent banking crises in Mexico and Venezuela have led the Mexican and Venezuelan governments to loosen restrictions on foreign entry, and there has been significant new entry by foreign banks into those countries. If the experiences of Argentina and New Zealand are any guide, Mexico and Venezuela should be able to achieve more politically credible discipline over their banks.

5
Conclusions

This volume has traced the development of the modern bank safety net, the growing disillusion with bank safety nets internationally over the past decade, and potential reforms to safety net policies, notably subordinated-debt requirements. Those requirements, I have argued, may point the way to a stable and incentive-compatible postmodern era of bank deregulation.

As the examples of Chilean and Argentine banking reforms illustrate, bringing credible private market discipline to bear on banks may allow developing countries to come to grips with the destabilizing influence of poorly managed safety nets. The challenge remains implementing a combination of policies that will allow banks to provide innovative and efficient financial services while avoiding perverse incentives to free ride on government protection. Despite some shortcomings in the policies of both countries, Chile and Argentina have been among the most committed regulatory innovators in the search for bank stability and efficiency.

References

Barth, James R., and Philip F. Bartholomew. 1992. "The Thrift Industry Crisis: Revealed Weaknesses in the Federal Deposit Insurance System." In *The Reform of Federal Deposit Insurance,* edited by James R. Barth and R. Dan Brumbaugh, Jr. New York: Harper Business, 36–116.

Boyd, John, and Mark Gertler. 1994. "The Role of Large Banks in the Recent U.S. Banking Crisis." *Federal Reserve Bank of Minneapolis Quarterly Review* (Winter): 2–21.

Brewer, Elijah III. 1995. "The Impact of the Current Deposit Insurance System on S&L Shareholders' Risk/Return Tradeoffs." *Journal of Financial Services Research* 9: 65–69.

Brewer, Elijah III, and Thomas Mondschean. 1993. "Junk Bond Holdings, Premium Tax Offsets, and Risk Exposure at Life Insurance Companies." Working paper 93-3, Federal Reserve Bank of Chicago.

Brewer, Elijah III, Thomas Mondschean, and Philip Strahan. 1992."The Effect of Capital on Portfolio Risk at Life Insurance Companies." Working paper 92-29, Federal Reserve Bank of Chicago.

Brock, Philip L., ed. 1992. *If Texas Were Chile: A Primer on Bank Reform.* San Francisco: ICS Press.

Budnevich, Carlos. 1996. "Banking System Regulation in Chile." Working paper, Banco Central de Chile.

Calomiris, Charles W. 1989. "Deposit Insurance: Lessons from the Record." *Federal Reserve Bank of Chicago Eco-*

nomic Perspectives (May/June): 10–30.

———. 1990. "Is Deposit Insurance Necessary? An Historical Perspective." *Journal of Economic History* 50: 283–95.

———. 1991. "The Motives of U.S. Debt Management Policy, 1790–1880: Efficient Discrimination and Time Consistency." *Research in Economic History* 13: 67–105.

———. 1992. "Do 'Vulnerable' Economies Need Deposit Insurance? Lessons from U.S. Agriculture in the 1920s." In *If Texas Were Chile: A Primer on Banking Reform*, edited by Philip Brock. San Francisco: ICS Press, 237–14.

———. 1993a. "The Decline of Private Deposit Insurance in the United States: A Comment." *Carnegie-Rochester Series on Public Policy* 38: 129–42.

———. 1993b. "Regulation, Industrial Structure, and Instability in U.S. Banking: An Historical Perspective." In *Structural Change in Banking*, edited by Michael Klausner and Lawrence J. White. Homewood, Ill.: Business One–Irwin, 19–116.

———. 1994. "Is the Discount Window Necessary? A Penn Central Perspective." *Federal Reserve Bank of St. Louis Review* 76 (May/June): 31–55.

———. 1997. "Building an Incentive-Compatible Safety Net: Special Problems for Developing Countries." *Journal of Banking and Finance*, forthcoming.

Calomiris, Charles W., and Gary Gorton. 1991. "The Origins of Banking Panics: Models, Facts, and Bank Regulation." In *Financial Markets and Financial Crises*, edited by R. Glenn Hubbard. Chicago: University of Chicago Press, 109–73.

Calomiris, Charles W., and Charles M. Kahn. 1991. "The Role of Demandable Debt in Structuring Optimal Banking Arrangements." *American Economic Review* 81 (June): 497–513.

Calomiris, Charles W., Charles M. Kahn, and Stefan Krasa.

1994. "Optimal Contingent Bank Liquidation under Moral Hazard." Working paper, Columbia University.

Calomiris, Charles W., and Joseph Mason. 1997. "Contagion and Bank Failures during the Great Depression: The June 1932 Chicago Banking Panic." *American Economic Review,* forthcoming.

Calomiris, Charles W., and Carlos D. Ramirez. 1996. "The Role of Financial Relationships in the History of American Corporate Finance." *Journal of Applied Corporate Finance* 9 (Summer): 52–73.

Calomiris, Charles W., and Larry Schweikart. 1991. "The Panic of 1857: Origins, Transmission, and Containment." *Journal of Economic History* 51 (December): 807–34.

Calomiris, Charles W., and David C. Wheelock. 1997. "Was the Great Depression a Watershed in American Monetary History?" In *The Defining Moment,* edited by Michael Bordo, Claudia Goldin, and Eugene White. Chicago: University of Chicago Press, forthcoming.

Calomiris, Charles W., and Eugene N. White. 1994. "The Origins of Federal Deposit Insurance." In *The Regulated Economy,* edited by Claudia Goldin and Gary Libecap. Chicago: University of Chicago Press, 145–88.

Calomiris, Charles W., and Berry Wilson. 1997. "Bank Capital and Portfolio Management: The 1930s Capital Crunch and Scramble to Shed Risk." Working paper, Columbia University.

Caprio, Gerard, and Daniela Klingebiel. 1996a. "Bank Insolvency: Bad Luck, Bad Policy, or Bad Banking." In *Annual World Bank Conference on Development Economics, 1996,* edited by Michael Bruno and Boris Pleskovic.

———. 1996b. "Bank Insolvency: Cross-Country Experience." World Bank policy research working paper 1620, July.

Carey, Mark S. 1990. "Feeding the Fad: The Federal Land Banks, Land Market Efficiency, and the Farm Credit

Crisis." Ph.D. diss., University of California, Berkeley.

de Krivoy, Ruth. 1995. "Lessons from Financial Crises: Evidence from Venezuela." *Proceedings of the 31st Annual Conference on Bank Structure and Competition,* Federal Reserve Bank of Chicago.

de la Cuadra, Sergio, and Salvador Valdes. 1992. "Myths and Facts about Financial Liberalization in Chile: 1974–1983." In *If Texas Were Chile: A Primer on Banking Reform,* edited by Philip Brock. San Francisco: ICS Press, 11–101.

Edwards, Franklin R. 1996. *The New Finance: Regulation and Financial Stability.* Washington, D.C.: AEI Press.

Flood, Mark. 1992. "The Great Deposit Insurance Debate." *Federal Reserve Bank of St. Louis Review* 76 (May/June): 51–77.

Garber, Peter. 1997. "Managing Risks to Financial Markets from Volatile Capital Flows: The Role of Prudential Regulation." Working paper, Brown University.

Gorton, Gary. 1985. "Clearing Houses and the Origin of Central Banking in the United States." *Journal of Economic History* 45 (June): 277–83.

Horvitz, Paul. 1992. "The Causes of Texas Bank and Thrift Failures." In *If Texas Were Chile: A Primer on Banking Reform,* edited by Philip Brock. San Francisco: ICS Press, 131–60.

Kane, Edward. 1989. *The S&L Insurance Mess: How Did It Happen?* Washington, D.C.: Urban Institute Press.

———. 1992. "The Incentive Incompatibility of Government-Sponsored Deposit Insurance Funds." In *The Reform of Federal Deposit Insurance,* edited by James R. Barth and R. Dan Brumbaugh, Jr. New York: Harper Business, 144–66.

Keehn, Silas. 1989. "Banking on the Balance: Powers and the Safety Net, A Proposal." Working paper, Federal Reserve Bank of Chicago.

Lindgren, Carl-Johan, Gillian Garcia, and Matthew I. Saal. 1996. *Bank Soundness and Macroeconomic Policy*. Washington, D.C.: International Monetary Fund.

Mason, Joseph. 1996. "The Effects of Reconstruction Finance Corporation Assistance to Banks during the Great Depression." Working paper, Office of the Comptroller of the Currency.

Miller, Geoffrey P. 1993. "Politics of Deposit Insurance Reform: The Case of Argentina." *University of Chicago Law School Roundtable 1993*: 129–52.

Ramirez, Guillermo, and Francisco Rosende. 1992. "Responding to Collapse: Chilean Banking Legislation after 1983." In *If Texas Were Chile: A Primer on Banking Reform,* edited by Philip Brock. San Francisco: ICS Press, 193–216.

Schumacher, Liliana. 1997. "The Causes of Bank Failures in Argentina during the Tequila Crisis." Working paper, Banco Central de la Republica Argentina.

Schwartz, Anna J. 1992. "The Misuse of the Fed's Discount Window." *Federal Reserve Bank of St. Louis Review* (September/October): 58–69.

Wall, Larry D. 1989. "A Plan for Reducing Future Deposit Insurance Losses: Puttable Subordinated Debt." *Federal Reserve Bank of Atlanta Economic Review* (July/August): 2–17.

About the Author

CHARLES W. CALOMIRIS is the Paul M. Montrone Professor of Finance and Economics at the Columbia University Graduate School of Business and an AEI visiting scholar. He is the director of the Program on Financial Institutions at the Columbia Business School and a research associate of the National Bureau of Economic Research. Mr. Calomiris is the author of numerous papers and books on financial institutions, financial economics, and financial history and is the recipient of a number of grants and awards in his field. He serves or has served as a consultant on financial regulation for the Federal Reserve Board; the Federal Reserve Banks of New York, Chicago, and St. Louis; the World Bank; the Central Bank of Argentina; and the governments of Mexico, El Salvador, and China.

www.ingramcontent.com/pod-product-compliance
Lightning Source LLC
Jackson TN
JSHW080855211224
75817JS00002B/67